FREEDOM SEEKER

A Creative Minds Biography

FREEDOM SEEKER

A Story about William Penn

by Gwenyth Swain

illustrated by Lisa Harvey

Carolrhoda Books, Inc./Minneapolis

Special thanks to J. William Frost, director of the Friends Historical Library, Swarthmore College, for his comments on the manuscript in progress.

Author's Note: Spelling, capitalization, and punctuation in quoted materials have been changed for ease of reading.

This book is available in two editions:
Library binding by Carolrhoda Books, Inc.,
   a division of Lerner Publishing Group
Soft cover by First Avenue Editions,
   an imprint of Lerner Publishing Group
241 First Avenue North
Minneapolis, MN 55401 U.S.A.

Website address: www.lernerbooks.com

Library of Congress Cataloging-in-Publication Data

Swain, Gwenyth, 1961–
    Freedom seeker: a story about William Penn / by Gwenyth Swain;
illustrations by Lisa Harvey.
        p.   cm. — (A creative minds biography)
    Includes bibliographical references and index.
    ISBN: 1–57505–176–1 (lib. bdg. : alk. paper)
    ISBN: 0–87614–931–X (pbk. : alk. paper)
    1. Penn, William 1644–1718—Juvenile literature. 2. Pioneers—
Pennsylvania—Biography—Juvenile literature. 3. Quakers—
Pennsylvania—Biography—Juvenile literature. 4. Pennsylvania—
History—Colonial period, ca. 1600–1775—Juvenile literature. [1. Penn,
William, 1644–1718. 2. Quakers. 3. Pennsylvania—History—Colonial
period, ca. 1600–1775.] I. Harvey, Lisa, ill. II. Title. III. Series.
F152.2 .S95 2003
974.8'02'092—dc21   2001000049

Manufactured in the United States of America
1 2 3 4 5 6 – JR – 08 07 06 05 04 03

Table of Contents

1

The Captain's Son

Just by being born—on October 14, 1644—
William Penn made his father happy. Like most parents, Captain William Penn was in a hurry. His ship,
the *Fellowship,* was waiting in the Thames River in
London, England. Captain Penn was waiting for orders from the navy to sail and waiting to finish his
business on land.

When the baby, named William after his father,
cried strong and loud, his mother, Margaret, let out a
sigh of relief. Thank goodness! A healthy baby, and
a boy at that. His father felt puffed up with joy. He
had an heir, a boy who might grow up to become a sea

captain like himself. Or perhaps something even grander—an ambassador or a minister of state.

On October 23, William was baptized in the Church of England. Soon afterward, Captain Penn got his orders and set sail. Young William didn't see his father again until the summer of 1646. By then, William could pull himself up the stone steps of the house his parents rented on Tower Hill in London. By then, his father had become a vice admiral.

At age twenty-four, William's father was already a rising star in the navy. But these were troubled times. Even a rising star could suddenly fall. While young William struggled to learn the name of his father's newest ship, the *Happy Entrance,* civil war was raging in England.

England's king, Charles I, never much cared for Parliament, the group of lords and elected men who helped govern the country. He would have ignored members of Parliament completely, but in 1642 they'd begun waging war against their king. Leading Parliament's army was a man named Oliver Cromwell. Cromwell wrested control of the navy away from the king. This made him Admiral Penn's commander.

William's father had been loyal to the king before the war, but that didn't stop him from being a good worker in Parliament's navy. In 1648, with the war still raging, one of Admiral Penn's friends joined the Royalists, the king's supporters. Just having a friend who was a Royalist was enough to make Cromwell and Parliament suspicious. In April Admiral Penn was locked in the Tower of London.

William was too young to understand what was happening, but he already knew plenty about the Tower. It was the biggest—and scariest—thing in his neighborhood. Built as a home for kings, the stone rooms and dungeons of the Tower had been converted into a prison long before William was born. Many people believed there were torture chambers down dark passageways lit by smoky torches. Tower guards were said to use torture devices such as the scavenger's daughter, the boot, the narrow-bore, the iron collar, and the pilliwinks, which squeezed the fingers.

William's father never got near the torture chambers. He was too good a sea captain for Cromwell and Parliament to hold him long without proof of disloyalty. Whatever Admiral Penn thought of Cromwell, he was wise enough to keep it to himself.

About the same time his father was in the Tower, William caught smallpox. On a London street in the 1600s, as many as half the faces in the crowd were scarred by smallpox blisters. The blisters made a person's skin feel as if it were on fire. Those who carried the scars were lucky. They had survived. Most people who caught the disease died of it, especially children. William was not quite four when he caught smallpox. He felt the fiery fever and the burning rash of the pox. In the end, he was a lucky one, losing only his hair, not his life.

William's father made sure his son had a wig. Then the admiral set about finding a new home for the family—in a neighborhood that didn't smell so much. In the years of the English Civil War, people had taken to throwing dead cats and dogs and rats into the moat around the Tower of London. It was quicker than trying to find a place to bury them. The bodies floated and rotted in the water that ringed the Tower.

In the Penns' neighborhood, the stench of decaying flesh mixed with the smell of emptied chamber pots. Garbage piled up in the streets. No one seemed to be in charge. When Admiral Penn learned about a house for rent in Wanstead, just north of London, he quickly moved his family there.

At Wanstead, William lived as a young country gentleman. Private tutors came to the house to teach him his letters and numbers until he was old enough to enroll at nearby Chigwell School. When William wasn't studying his Latin, reading the Bible, or adding and subtracting, he was out in the sun. Soon his hair grew back. He didn't have to wear a wig when he first met his little sister, Peg, born in 1650.

The Penns should have lived a quiet, happy life at Wanstead. But England was in an uproar. A year before Peg Penn was born, King Charles I finally lost his battle with Parliament. In London, a special court found the king guilty of treason. The court declared that he had betrayed the trust that English people had in him as their king. And for that, Charles I lost his head. Executioners always held a guilty man's head up high, saying "So perish all the King's enemies. Behold the head of a traitor." Then the crowds would rush forward to catch the dripping blood in their handkerchiefs. But this was different. The king had been executed. Many people in England weren't sure what to think when Oliver Cromwell began ruling the country.

Cromwell sent Admiral Penn to track down what was left of the Royalist fleet. William didn't see his father again until the spring of 1651. The seven-year-old boy tugged at his mother's sleeve as they walked along the Thames River in London. As the captain's family, the Penns were rowed from shore to the bobbing *Fairfax*. The ship was filled with treasures Admiral Penn had captured from the Royalists. Five great trunks filled with silver and gold were lifted onto the deck from the *Fairfax's* hold—all to be given to Cromwell and Parliament.

Cromwell was happy enough with Penn's work to make him vice admiral of the entire English fleet. It was an important job, but it was bound to keep William's father away from England for months—or even years—at a time. How could a boy get to know a man who seemed to spend most of his time saying good-bye?

From the little time he'd spent with the admiral, William knew that his father was different from him. Like his mother, William's father loved to laugh, to eat and drink well, and to join friends for jokes or card games late into the night. Try as he might to be like his father, William fell short. He couldn't help what he was—a serious, quiet boy.

When William read the Bible at Chigwell School, he really *read* it, thinking it through and memorizing it without even trying. He didn't stop with the Bible. William devoured nearly every book he could find. He did other things well enough: he learned to bow and to dance from the dancing master his parents hired to train him in gentlemanly manners. He loved riding his family's horses. Yet even the best afternoon on horseback was dull compared to thinking about things he had read.

On brief visits home, Admiral Penn was pleased to learn that his son was doing well in school. A fair amount of book learning never hurt a gentleman, as long as he also knew how to handle a horse and to bow with the proper flourish. Admiral Penn was satisfied, even though the boy seemed a bit gloomy.

Before long, the whole family was gloomy. In 1654 Cromwell sent Admiral Penn to the Americas. William's father was ordered to capture the island of Hispaniola from Spain. He failed to do that, but he captured the island of Jamaica instead. The admiral had learned it was best to return with something, even if it meant not following orders to the letter. But Cromwell was not pleased. In September 1655, Admiral Penn was jailed in the Tower. William, Peg, and their mother crowded into rented rooms on Tower Hill.

Would Cromwell allow an admiral who disobeyed orders to rejoin the navy? Would the admiral write a full apology, or "letter of submission," to Cromwell, as everyone suggested? Or would he sit in prison for years and years? Admiral Penn's answer must have made William proud. Instead of writing a "letter of submission," he merely apologized for returning without awaiting orders. It was enough to get William's father released from the Tower. It was not enough to give him back his navy command.

In 1656 the Penns headed for Ireland. In happier times, Cromwell had given them an estate there called Macroom, complete with a castle. It was just the place to retreat to if you had fallen out of favor in dangerous times.

William Penn was almost twelve years old when he moved to Ireland. Every day, the clicking of his father's boot heels sounded in the stone halls of Macroom Castle. Mr. Penn 13 his new son Richard, or Dick, born that same year. He called out orders to servants, rode his horse along the Sullane River, and talked with the Irish people who farmed his land.

Some days William felt as if he were reading a new and fascinating book, all about his father. He could only guess what Mr. Penn had been like striding up and down the decks of ships. At Macroom, William's father revealed himself in large and small ways.

Thrusting and parrying, William's father tested and trained his son in how to fight with a sword. Strength and concentration were important, but so was confidence. While his father shouted encouragement, William kept practicing until he could fight as well as any swordsman.

William learned other lessons from the fights his father did *not* pick. William expected his father to dislike the odd fellow named Thomas Loe who was traveling across Ireland trying to interest people in his religion. Loe was one of the people known as Seekers of Truth, Children of Love, or Quakers—people who held religious views that many thought outlandish. According to Quakers, people didn't need a priest to tell them God's word. God spoke directly to all hearts ready to listen. That notion was enough to make priests in the Church of England hate Quakers.

Quakers also ignored some social customs. When they passed a lord in the street, Quakers didn't bow and take off their hats, as was the custom. In their shops, they didn't haggle with customers over prices, insisting that the prices they set were fair. They even talked funny, using the informal *thou* instead of the more proper *you*. (At that time, *thee* and *thou* were used only to address servants, children, and people who were considered socially inferior.)

So it surprised William when Mr. Penn invited Thomas Loe to the castle. William's father, having heard a little about the Quakers, said he wanted to hear more before he judged them. After a good dinner and some talk about religion, Loe held what Quakers called a *meeting*.

If William hadn't known before that *meeting* was the Quaker word for religious service, he wouldn't have been able to describe just what happened that night. They were all there but the younger children: William's mother, his father, his tutor, and even the family's black servant, a slave his father had brought home from Jamaica. Together, they sat without speaking until Thomas Loe rose to his feet.

Loe had listened intently, quietly. He believed the voice of God was speaking to him, and when he stood he shared the words he had heard. It was unlike anything William had ever experienced. Loe spoke of inward light, and it seemed to William that the man's face glowed as if it were lit from within. William looked around the room. His father's black slave was sobbing. Mr. Penn was silent, but William saw tears falling down his cheeks.

Thomas Loe left Macroom Castle without converting, or as the Quakers put it, *convincing* anyone in the household to join his strange religion. As far as William could tell, his father was just the same as ever—fair and open and friendly—despite those stray tears. But Loe's visit had planted questions in William's mind: What power could create such warmth in his heart? What power could make the lord of a castle and a former admiral cry in front of his family and servants?

2

Radical Notions

Events crowded out William's questions. In the fall of 1658, Oliver Cromwell died, and Parliament struggled to run the country. Even respectable people dared to say *out loud* that they wished they were ruled by a king. With no king or other strong leader, the English government bobbed about aimlessly, a ship without a captain. When Parliament decided to ask Charles Stuart—the old king's son—to return, it chose William's father to find Stuart in Holland and bring him home.

The former admiral had always seemed faithful to Cromwell. But his true loyalties became clear the minute Charles Stuart stepped onto the deck of the

Naseby. In his first act as England's new king, Charles II pulled out his sword and, tapping it lightly on both shoulders, made Mr. Penn a knight. Charles II also put Penn in charge of the Royal Navy, serving under his brother the duke of York. William's father had become Admiral Sir William Penn.

In 1660 William and his family moved back to their old neighborhood on Tower Hill. This time the family lived in a large house on Seething Lane near the navy office, where Sir William worked. People started cleaning up the Tower, but it took a while for the stink to go away. On days when the wind blew from the navy's slaughterhouse, William wished he were anywhere but home.

He got his wish in October, when the city looked as gray as the skies above. William was sixteen years old, and his father was sending him to college. He enrolled at Christ Church College, Oxford, that fall and began studying and reading with his usual hunger.

At first, when fellow students asked William to join them for a night of card games and ale, he wondered how they finished their studies so quickly. He was only halfway through the first book in the great pile he was to read! Gradually, he saw that most of his classmates had time *only* for fun and games and drinking—and for shouting late at night when they came back to their rooms at the college.

They seemed mostly interested in show. They showed up at lectures and showed themselves to be at least half-awake. And even though they rarely studied, they showed the world they were students by wearing the surplice, a knee-length top with large sleeves. It was the kind of top that priests in the Church of England wore. All students had to wear a surplice and attend chapel services.

William didn't mind following rules when they made sense, but he thought wearing the surplice and going to chapel were just part of the show. And the show had nothing to do with real learning and study. William probably skipped more chapel services than he should have. After the first time or two, his excuses for not wearing his surplice wore thin with the professors at Christ Church College.

When William came home for a visit, his parents should have worried about his behavior. But they and all of London were too busy getting ready for a party. On April 23, 1661, Charles Stuart would be officially crowned king.

That spring London looked scrubbed and smelled sweet, especially on the day before the coronation. William and his father rose early. They wore embroidered vests and velvet coats and made sure the lacy tops of their stockings flowed out, just so, over the tops of their high leather boots. Together with a few neighbors, the Penns went to a home on the king's parade route, where they had rented a room for the day. The street below was freshly graveled, and even the horses in the parade were well dressed. The best part of the day came when Charles II and the duke passed by the Penns' open window. With all of London wanting to be noticed, the king and his brother nodded and smiled to the Penns.

It was just the kind of thing Sir William had been hoping for. Being noticed by the king could give a young man's career a great boost. But when William again returned from school in March 1662, he seemed intent on spoiling his father's well-laid plans. William Penn had been thrown out of Oxford. He had been skipping chapel and wearing whatever he chose. William had also been attending religious services at the home of a professor who had been fired for radical notions, or beliefs.

In the 1660s, notions that got English people into trouble were usually related to religion. Officially, England had one church, the Church of England. English people had to go to services at least once every Sunday. If they didn't, they faced a one-shilling fine. It wasn't a lot of money, but it added up quickly.

Despite the threat of a fine, many religious groups held services in England. Along with the Quakers William remembered from Ireland, there were Roman Catholics, Baptists, and a host of others, most of whom met in secret.

Because Charles II had spent many years in Catholic countries, such as France and Spain, Parliament viewed him with suspicion—even though he was the official head of the Church of England. Charles II might have wanted to let Catholics and other "nonconformists," as they were called, hold services as they wished. But if he wanted to remain king, he had to do as Parliament wished. Parliament wished to show no mercy to nonconformists.

When William came home from Oxford in the spring of 1662, his father gave him a good whipping and kicked him out the door. (Lady Penn, Peg, and young Dick called William back as soon as the coast was clear.) Admiral Penn was still angry when he put William on a ship bound for France.

By July William was strolling the streets of Paris. There, his father hoped William might forget religion and pick up some polish. William did improve his French and also gained a new wardrobe in the latest Paris style. But one night made him remember his days at Oxford. William was heading back to his rooms, hugging the walls of the houses, just in case someone chose to dump a chamber pot out the window. A man passed going the other way, but it was too dark for William to see. He only knew it was a gentleman when the man pulled out his sword, demanding that William take off his hat or fight to the death.

The man must have taken off his own hat first, but in the dark William hadn't seen a thing. When William didn't remove his hat and bow, too, he had insulted the gentleman—and such an insult demanded a duel. A few minutes later, standing over the man and resting a sword point not too lightly on his chest, William caught his breath. Could anyone in his right mind, he wondered, think the custom of taking off hats was worth one's life?

William jumped away, letting the man scramble for his sword and scurry down the street. He was happy to let the fight end that way, but he couldn't let go of the question so easily. To William, taking off one's hat to honor another person was another kind of show. Just as putting on a surplice showed that one was a student, removing a hat showed the world one was a gentleman. But what really made someone a gentleman? There was no bravery in fighting over a simple misunderstanding. There was little honor in doffing hats when it was too dark for anyone to see.

William did not stay long in Paris. He had heard of a school in Saumur, a few days' ride from the city. There, in the heart of Catholic France, was the Protestant Academy, and there, too, was Moses Amyraut, a teacher who believed in religious tolerance. In 1663 William not only studied with Amyraut, he also lived in his house. With all its beauty and charm, France hadn't managed to make William forget about religion.

Within months, William's father called him home. The English, Sir William feared, would soon be at war with the Dutch. William would be safer back home in England.

3

War, Plague, and Light

When father and son met again on Tower Hill in the fall of 1664, they did their best to avoid talking about religion. That wasn't too hard since so much was going on around them. The neighborhood around the Tower always bustled, but while England's navy prepared for war, it hummed.

William tagged along with his father at work. How was shipbuilding going at the navy docks? Were there going to be enough sailors to fight a war? Would there be enough money to pay them? From time to time, Sir William dipped into his own pocket to keep the sailors fed while they waited in ships on the Thames River.

William was sad to leave home again in February 1665, but he agreed with his father that it was time he took up some work of his own. At age twenty, he entered law school at Lincoln's Inn on the other side of London. William's law books were a far cry from the religious works he'd been reading up to then. But he took to them with the same eagerness he brought to the Bible, memorizing whole passages.

William probably never meant to become a lawyer. Learning a bit of the law—like going to Oxford or studying French—was good training for a government minister or an ambassador. It couldn't beat learning on the job, however. When England finally waged war against Holland that spring, William left school. For a few weeks, he was his father's unofficial assistant at the navy office and onboard ship. He even carried a message from the fleet to the king. When Charles II heard that young William Penn had brought the message, he insisted on talking with him. "Oh, is it you?" the king asked. "How is Sir William?"

William told his father every detail. Soon afterward, William returned safely to law school, doing his best to settle back into student life. But he worried about his father. "I pray God," he wrote, "after all the foul weather and dangers you are exposed to, and shall be, that you come home as secure. . . . It's hard, meantime, to lose both a father and a friend."

William Penn would soon think his father lucky to be at sea—far, far away from England. London had known outbreaks of the plague before, so people didn't panic at the start of this one. By June 1665, however, one hundred people had died in a single week. That's when the Inns of Court, where William watched lawyers argue cases, shut down. At Lincoln's Inn, visitors were looked over closely for swellings, spots, and blotches that came with the horrible disease. By July all schools in the city closed, and William went home to Tower Hill.

People with the plague were supposed to stay shut up in their homes. A large red cross—and sometimes the words "Lord have mercy"—was painted on the door. Doctors believed the disease spread from one person to another, so healthy people went out as little as possible. When William dashed down the street to shop, others looked at him in fear. Would he be the one to give them the plague? The Penn's next-door neighbor, Samuel Pepys, wrote in his diary, "[S]o many poor sick people in the streets, full of sores, and so many sad stories overheard as I walk, everybody talking of this dead, and that man sick, and so many in this place, and so many in that."

That fall city leaders lit bonfires on nearly every street, hoping the fires' heat might somehow cleanse the air and stop the dying. Many houses stood empty, red paint glowing in the firelight. William Penn turned twenty-one while tens of thousands were dying around him. He couldn't imagine how or why he and his family had been spared. He wondered if it was God's will that he survive the plague just so he could go to Ireland. When his father asked him to go there early in 1666, he did.

Shanagarry Castle was a gift to Sir William from the king, but its original owner had filed a lawsuit to get it back. Because of his law studies, William was sent to settle the suit. He quickly took care of the lawsuit, but he still had much work to do. He rode over acres of countryside to meet farmers who worked the land. At the castle, he had servants to direct.

William kept at his work in Ireland, even when a great fire nearly burned the whole city of London in September. Once again, the Penns were spared, although the flames and showers of sparks came so close that Sir William dug a hole in the backyard to bury his wine. Once again, it seemed God had put the Penns out of harm's way. For what purpose? William wondered.

He was still puzzling over that question late in the summer of 1667, when he stopped in a shop in Cork to buy some cloth. The shop owner was a Quaker, so William told her about meeting Thomas Loe years earlier. If he knew where Loe was preaching, William went on, he would go a hundred miles just to hear him. You needn't go that far, the shopkeeper assured him. Thomas Loe would be at a meeting in Cork the very next day. William had only to stay to hear him.

When William came the next day, he was given a seat just like any other Quaker. He knew that Quakers rose from their benches when they heard God's message. William sat with the others for a short time. He wasn't surprised when Thomas Loe stood up and gave them all a message. He wasn't surprised to feel warmth in his heart as Loe spoke. But William was surprised when he felt his own legs pull him up. It was as if a voice inside him had said, "Stand on thy feet!" When he stood, he could find no words, only tears. The voice told him to keep standing. "How dost thou know but somebody may be reach'd by thy tears?"

From that moment on, William was one of the Quakers, or Friends, as they called themselves. He couldn't have chosen a worse time to become a Quaker. Of all the nonconformists in England, Quakers were the most laughed at and least tolerated. When Parliament passed laws against nonconformists, most met in secret and spoke in whispers.

But Quakers didn't. Everything about them shouted out loud that they were Quakers—even though it was against the law to be members of anything but the Church of England.

Although William knew from his first meeting in Cork that he was one of the Friends, it took him a while to fit in. For example, William wore a sword, which clattered when he sat down in meeting. But Friends did not believe in using violence or carrying weapons. When a soldier broke up one meeting, William grabbed the man by the collar. He would have thrown the soldier down the stairs if other Friends hadn't stopped him. The soldier came back with reinforcements and arrested several Friends, including William. At court the magistrate insisted there must be a mistake—a gentleman such as William could not be a Quaker. Whether or not you think so, William told the magistrate, I'm one of them. And if you're sending other Friends to prison, I'm going, too.

As William was led into prison, he bowed to his servant and gave him his sword. All of William's Quaker friends had given up some part of their past lives—wealth, family, jobs, homes—when they became Quakers. William was leaving his old life behind. He didn't need to be armed where he was going.

William's usual stream of letters to his family about matters at Shanagarry had slowed down to a mere trickle. Sir William was concerned, not just by William's silence but by some unsettling rumors he'd heard. "Son William," he wrote, "I have writ several letters to you since I received any from you. By this I again charge you & strictly command that you come to me with all possible speed. . . . Your affectionate father, W. Penn."

William hated to displease his father, but he could not return home until he was out of jail. When he was finally released in November, he saddled his horse and headed home. The William Penn who arrived at his parents' doorstep did not look much different from the William Penn they had last seen earlier in the year. Word spread fast, however, that he was a changed man. Next door, Mr. Pepys wrote in his diary that a Mrs. Turner had been to visit. "Among other talk," he wrote, "she tells me that Mr. Will Pen[n], who is lately come over from Ireland, is a Quaker again, or some very melancholy thing."

What was gossip to the neighbors was tragedy to Sir William. How many years of his life had he spent preparing his oldest son for a brilliant career? How could young William throw away such opportunity and act as if nothing was lost?

When William refused to remove his hat to honor his father, Sir William cried out. Hadn't he raised his son better than this? When William used the more familiar term *thou* when talking to his father, Sir William despaired. Such bad manners!

At that time in England, it was customary to use the more formal *you* when talking to someone more important or older than oneself. But it was also customary to use the more familiar *thou* when praying to God. William didn't think mere men should be treated more formally than God. If he used *thou* when speaking with everyone he met, he was telling them that they were all equal. And he believed they were capable of finding God's light within themselves, just as he had done among the Friends.

Sir William said, you can "thee" and "thou" as much as you please, but don't do it with me or the king or the duke of York. He didn't add that using thee and thou with the king might cause William to lose his head. William understood the danger. His father hinted that the two of them would be making a visit to the court of Charles II the next morning. William didn't sleep all night.

The coach that came for him and Sir William the next morning drove into a park, far from the king's palace. William realized they weren't truly going to court.

Even then, he struggled to be calm. This disagreement with his father had to be discussed openly.

He reminded his father of his own tears years before when Thomas Loe spoke at the castle. Hadn't Sir William been at least a little bit convinced then that the Quaker was speaking the truth?

When they'd talked so long they couldn't ignore their thirst, the men carried their conversation into a nearby tavern. In a private room, Sir William tried one more time to save his son. With shaking hands resting on the table, he told William he was prepared to get down on his knees. God, he'd pray, please don't make my son a Quaker!

William ran to the window, answering that he would throw himself out onto the cobbled street below before he would listen to such a prayer. Father and son were at a standoff. Only their grief brought them together. While Sir William mourned the loss of his son's great future, William grieved for the pain he'd brought to his father and friend.

4

"I Know the Way to Newgate"

William left home again in 1668. As much he hated to leave his family behind, his life was elsewhere, among Friends. He traveled from town to town in England, visiting with Friends and joining them at meetings. As William traveled, he learned of the many Quakers who had been imprisoned for following their religion. Despite the joy he felt in his heart since becoming a Friend, William was saddened to think of such suffering.

Soon he was gaining firsthand knowledge of what it meant to suffer as a Friend. That fall, William wrote a religious booklet in which he tried to respond to critics of the Quakers. Because he wrote too fast and sloppily, William's words were misunderstood. Not long before Christmas, William Penn was locked in the Tower of London. The official charge was publishing a religious work without first getting the approval of the bishop of London. But the real reason for Penn's arrest lay in his ideas about religion—ideas the bishop would never have approved. Even the man who had published the booklet was sent to jail.

William was horrified that he'd caused a man to be put in prison. But he wasn't sorry for what he'd written. When a rare visitor was allowed into his small cell, William spoke confidently, "Thou mayst tell my father, whom, I know, will ask thee, these words, that my prison shall be my grave before I will budge a jot."

Over the winter, William shivered in the poorly heated room, but his heart was warm and his mind overflowing with ideas. By candlelight he worked slowly and steadily on his newest booklet. He wasn't going to make the same mistake twice. In *No Cross, No Crown,* William carefully gathered quotes from the Bible plus stories from history and his own life. If people wanted to gain the crown of God's "love, peace, [and] joy," then they would have to carry a cross. William wasn't talking about a real cross. He was talking about the sacrifices he and others had made when they became Friends.

Those sacrifices weren't easy to bear. "God often touches our best comforts," William explained, "and calls for that which we most love, and are least willing to part with . . . I speak [from] my experience." But once people decide to live new lives as Friends, William went on, "light shines in their souls, and thereby gives them a sight of their sins." William believed that light was God's love and understanding. This belief allowed William and others to see what they had done wrong in the past and to try to do better in the future. To many readers, the life William described in *No Cross, No Crown* sounded gloomy. To William, it was the only life worth living.

Through winter and summer, William wrote on. His hair fell out from the extremes of hot and cold. Late in July 1669, William was finally let out of the Tower, but he didn't stay clear of trouble for long.

About a year later, William and another Friend, William Mead, were on trial for preaching outside a Quaker meetinghouse on London's Gracious Street. Soldiers had nailed the doors shut, so Penn and Mead held a meeting on the street. They waited until Penn spoke before arresting him and Mead.

Standing before a packed courtroom on September 1, 1670, John Howell, the court recorder, read the charges "that William Penn, gent. and William Mead, late of London, linen-draper . . . unlawfully and tumultuously did assemble and congregate themselves together, to the disturbance of the peace." Howell went on, saying that Penn "in the open street, did take upon himself to preach and speak."

The first day of the trial started badly. Penn and Mead had lost their hats in the scuffle on Gracious Street. William Starling, lord mayor of London, wanted some fun. Weren't Quakers fanatics about wearing hats? From the bench, he asked, "Who bid you put off their hats? Put on their hats again." An officer put hats on the prisoners, and the lord mayor promptly fined Penn and Mead for wearing hats in court.

Penn shot back that "not we, but the bench, should be fined." Howell called Penn "saucy" and "impertinent," but the trial went on. When witnesses were called to the stand, they all said they couldn't hear what Penn had said in Gracious Street. If no one heard him, how could he be charged with nonconformist preaching? Penn asked.

"My lord," Howell told Mayor Starling, "if you take not some course with this pestilent fellow, to stop his mouth, we shall not be able to do anything tonight."

Mead didn't get any better treatment. When he tried to defend himself, the lord mayor said, "You deserve to have your tongue cut out."

Mead answered, "Thou didst promise me I should have fair liberty to be heard. Why may I not have the privilege of an Englishman?"

The court did its best to "stop the mouths" of Penn and Mead, but the men had already won over some of the jury. When the lord mayor asked for a verdict, jurors first split eight to four, then decided that Penn was "guilty of speaking in Gracious Street."

"Is that all?" The lord mayor was astounded. To him it was obvious that Penn was guilty of much worse. But the jury answered that they could find no evidence that Penn had done anything more. Mead was not found guilty of any charge. Howell was outraged. "Gentlemen," he told the jury, "you shall not be dismissed, till we have a verdict that the court will accept; and you shall be locked up, without meat, drink, fire and tobacco. . . . [W]e will have a verdict, by the help of God, or you shall starve for it."

Court officials in the 1600s often told juries how they should rule in cases. Sometimes they locked up juries that didn't follow orders. But this jury was different. They listened when Penn asked, "What hope is there of ever having justice done, when juries are threatened, and their verdicts rejected?" They saw the logic in Penn's defense: "[I]f William Mead be not guilty, it consequently follows, that I am clear; since you have indicted us of a conspiracy, and I could not possibly conspire alone."

When the jury returned with its final verdict, it found both Mead and Penn not guilty of any charge. Howell chided the jury. "I am sorry, gentlemen," he said, "that you have followed your own judgments and opinions, rather than the good and wholesome advice which was given you. . . . [F]or this the court fines you forty marks a man, and imprisonment till paid." Penn asked if he and Mead were free, but he had forgotten the lord mayor's hat fine. Together, defendants and jury were taken to Newgate Prison until their fines were paid.

The case might have stopped there. But Penn and Mead and some of the jurors refused or were unable to pay their fines. When the jurors appealed to a higher court, the judge ruled in their favor, dismissing the jurors' fines. He agreed that it was, just as Penn had argued, a fundamental right of Englishmen to have a fair jury trial.

William Penn had little chance to savor his victory. His father was dying. Knowing his son's stubbornness, Sir William paid the hat fine. "Son William, I am weary of the world," the old admiral admitted. He died just one week later, still disappointed, but having made peace with his son. Sir William left his son a large estate and another gift worth much, much more. Before his death, Sir William had written to the king and the duke of York asking them, as friends, to look out for his wayward son. But kings and dukes could do only so much to help a young man who seemed bent on breaking the law.

In February 1671, William Penn was again arrested for nonconformist preaching. This time the charge didn't call for a jury trial. The man sentencing Penn was an old neighbor, Sir John Robinson, keeper of the Tower.

"Is your name Penn?" Robinson asked.

"Dost thou not know me? Hast thou forgot me?" Penn asked in turn.

"I do not know you," Robinson answered. "I do not desire to know such as you are." Robinson didn't want to waste time talking to a Quaker. "Well," he said, "I must send you to Newgate for six months."

"Is that all?" Penn asked. "Thou well knowest a larger imprisonment has not daunted me."

"Send a corporal," Robinson called, "with a file of musketeers along with him."

"No, no," Penn said. He needed no guards with muskets to escort him. "I know the way to Newgate."

5

A New Kind of Government

William may have known the way to Newgate, but he didn't know how awful the prison was. Another prisoner recalled, "When we first came into Newgate there lay . . . the quartered bodies of three men who had been executed some days before." Six months was a long time to live next to the dead and the dying. The Tower of London was free of "jail fever," but this horrible form of typhus struck hundreds of prisoners in Newgate. They shook with the fever and called out—or screamed.

The sick and the dying slept on dried rushes gathered from marshes or from the banks of the Thames. They lay on bundles of damp straw thrown onto the rat-infested floor. The luckier prisoners climbed over the others and tried to rock themselves to a troubled sleep in dirty hammocks. Daylight brought some relief. Healthier prisoners could work in a room on the second floor. All prisoners in those days had to pay for their keep, so work was vital. Penn, too, had work to do.

In his newest booklet, *The Great Case of Liberty of Conscience,* Penn argued that people should be free to practice whatever religion they wanted. To Penn, the same English law that guaranteed a trial by jury also promised freedom of religion. Other people simply weren't reading the law as he did. But more importantly, Penn thought that granting religious freedom was good common sense.

When a ruler—king or Parliament—told people to change their religion, the ruler was asking people to be untrue to themselves and to their God. How could you hope to govern people who were forced to lie? Penn asked. He argued that putting limits on religious freedom was unpatriotic. It tore at the very heart of a nation.

Penn and other Friends refused to lie or to hide their beliefs. As a result, Penn wrote, "to this time we labor under the unspeakable pressure of nasty prisons, and daily confiscation of our goods, to the apparent ruin of entire families."

While Penn labored in nasty Newgate, hoping his words would persuade Charles II, he also wrote letters to friends. Surely some of those letters were to Guli Springett, a young woman he had met a few years earlier. When his six-month stay at Newgate was over in July 1671, Penn went to see Guli straight away.

Guli was beside him that August when Penn went to London to see off George Fox, the founder of Quakerism. Fox was on his way to England's colonies in the New World. For years he had searched for a church to join. Finally, he created his own movement when he started preaching in 1647. Fox had none of Penn's great learning or fine manners, yet he drew people to him wherever he preached.

A few months later, a group of Quakers and others gathered in a home near London to attend a wedding. All the guests signed the marriage certificate, as is the Quaker custom. The certificate declared: "These are now to certify all persons to whom it doth or may concern, that upon the fourth day of the second month in the year one thousand six hundred seventy-two, the said William Penn and Gulielma Maria Springett, did, in a godly sort & manner . . . solemnly and expressly take each other in marriage, mutually promising to be loving, true & faithful." In Guli, William found a true friend as well as a wife.

The Penns lived well. William had inherited his father's estates, and Guli herself was an heiress. Yet even as his family grew (Guli was soon expecting a child), even as Friends gathered at his house, William could see that most Quakers weren't so lucky.

He did what he could to help those in prison and those who faced bankruptcy from fines. "Several families are well nigh ruined," William wrote the king, "their houses laid waste." The king seemed sympathetic. The duke of York called Quakers "a quiet industrious people" and told William that he was "against all persecution for the sake of religion." But Parliament still viewed nonconformists harshly. When Charles II issued a Declaration of Indulgence in 1672, freeing many Quakers, Parliament struck it down just months later.

William could see no hope of having freedom of religion in England. He wondered if the New World might not be a better place to plant the seeds of freedom and watch them grow. In 1674 William helped settle a dispute between a group of Quakers who owned a large tract of land in America called West New Jersey. The whole business was a headache, but it taught William how to draft laws.

In 1675 Guli gave birth to a "large & active" boy, and the couple named him Springett for Guli's family.

Three years later, a girl named Letitia, or Tish, joined the family at Worminghurst, near England's southern coast. The Penns' home in Worminghurst was, as William put it "very large, but ugly." The couple had room to welcome more than twenty overnight guests at a time, and they did. In the large but ugly hall, nearly two hundred Quakers could worship on Sundays. But still, William wondered if he could not do more for Friends.

If he had land of his own, where freedom and liberty were guaranteed, William knew Quakers would flock to it. In late May or early June 1680, William Penn sent a petition to the king. He asked for land in the New World, west of the Delaware River and between the colonies of Maryland and New York. It might have seemed outrageous to ask for so much. But years earlier, William's father had helped the king. During tough times, Admiral Sir William Penn had stocked ships in the king's navy with biscuits, pork, and drinking water, paying for everything with his own money.

Many wealthy Englishmen "loaned" money to the king when his expenses outstripped his income. Most never expected to be repaid. Surely Sir William had never expected to see again the thousands of pounds he'd spent feeding the Royal Navy.

By granting Sir William's son a gift of land, King Charles II might just be repaying an old friend. But such a gift could mean much more. By giving William Penn land in America, the king might finally rid England of the many Quakers who filled his country's jails. Once in the New World, they could sort out rules about religious freedom as they wished. Parliament was unlikely to interfere. Perhaps Charles II also remembered the promise he'd made to Sir William to watch out for his wayward son. Even though William Penn was a grown man of thirty-five, he hadn't yet learned to stay out of trouble. Only luck had kept him out of prison for the last few years.

Petitions to the king arrived at the palace at Whitehall in bundles. They usually sat there for years before getting an answer. William Penn got his answer on March 4, 1681. The king gave him a new colony in America. It would be called Pennsylvania— *Penn* for Sir William and *sylvania* for wooded land. Charles II insisted on the name as a way of honoring his old friend. William hated it, believing most people would assume he'd named the place after himself. He even tried bribing the king's secretary but couldn't get the man to change the name.

Soon William started the long, hard task of building Pennsylvania. His first step was to advertise. In a booklet William wrote and sent to Quakers in 1681, he described Pennsylvania as being "600 miles nearer the sun than England." He told future Pennsylvanians how much land would cost and what the fees were for passage by ship to America: "for masters and mistresses at most to £6 a head, for servants £5 a head, and for children under seven years of age, fifty shillings, except they suck [breast-feed], then nothing." Travel to Pennsylvania was not cheap. (Translated into modern terms, £6 is equal to just under one thousand dollars.)

But Penn was very persuasive. He had always been a good letter writer, keeping in touch with Friends in England and Europe. He wrote to as many as he could about Pennsylvania. "God . . . will, I believe, bless and make it the seed of a nation," Penn wrote in one letter. "I shall have a tender care to the government, that it be well laid at first."

Over the winter of 1681 and 1682, Penn turned his "tender care" to shaping the government of Pennsylvania. He wrote to the few thousand settlers already living in Pennsylvania, saying "you shall be governed by laws of your own making. . . . I shall not usurp the right of any." He wrote to the area's original inhabitants, the Lenni-Lenape Indians, promising that he and the people who came with him would "be examples of justice and goodness." Penn meant to create a place, he said, where "the will of one man may not hinder the good of a whole country."

It was a tall order. Penn had to imagine a kind of government that had never before existed. What he created was a mix of old and new government and law. Pennsylvania would have a governor (Penn or his heirs), who acted a bit like an old-fashioned large landowner in England. He expected the early settlers, called First Purchasers, to pay him rent, just as farmers on his family estates did. Yet he also made sure that all free male citizens of Pennsylvania could vote. In England, a man had to own land and be a citizen before he could hope to cast a vote. Penn also gave the Assembly and Council (similar to England's Parliament) the power to write and vote on laws.

Penn described his plan in a booklet called *The Frame of Government,* published in 1682. In other booklets, he outlined Pennsylvania's laws. Some laws seemed to rise out of Penn's own experience. One law declared that "all courts shall be open, and justice shall neither be sold, denied, nor delayed." Another law stated that "all persons living in this province who confess and acknowledge the one almighty and eternal God . . . shall in no way be molested or prejudiced for their religious persuasion."

Other laws went beyond anything Penn had ever experienced. Penn proposed that "all children within the province of the age of twelve years shall be taught some useful trade or skill, to the end that none may be idle, but the poor may work to live, and the rich, if they become poor, may not want." In Pennsylvania new settlers would resolve any differences with the Lenni-Lenape in a jury trial. "[A]ll differences between the planters and the natives," Penn noted, "shall also be ended by twelve men, that is, by six planters and six natives; that so we may live friendly together."

By the time Penn had finished the frame of government and laws, two ships filled with First Purchasers had already reached Pennsylvania. It was time for the governor to follow. Guli and a few close friends went with William for several miles along the road to Deal where the *Welcome* lay in harbor. Penn's wife and children—Springett, Tish, and the baby, Bille—would not be going with him. Guli's mother was ill, and Guli herself was pregnant and not fit for a long ocean voyage.

William Penn knew the dangers of travel by sea. He remembered, too, how he had felt as a child when his father left for months and years at a time. So before leaving Worminghurst, Penn wrote to all his children, starting with his oldest son:

My Dear Springett:

Be good, learn to fear God, avoid evil, love thy book, be kind to thy brother and sister, and God will bless thee and I will exceedingly love thee. Farewell dear child,

Thy dear father,

Wm Penn

My love to all the family and to Friends.

Penn brought well-packed trunks and a heart filled with love onto the *Welcome*. His ship was bigger than the *Mayflower*—the ship that had carried the first Pilgrims to America in 1620—yet it was still crowded, grimy, and damp. Penn and his fellow travelers made good time. But before long, many passengers fell ill. Smallpox spread through the ship, killing thirty-one people. Because Penn had survived smallpox as a child, he was immune to the illness. He spent much of the two-month voyage nursing the sick.

Late in October 1682, Penn paced the ship's deck and caught a hint of land. "[T]he air," he wrote, "smelled as sweet as a garden new blown." On October 28th, he made landfall at New Castle, in Delaware. From there, the *Welcome* made its way slowly up the Delaware River. The next time Penn got off the ship, he would be stepping on Pennsylvania soil.

6

Penn's Land

The *Welcome* traveled as far as the town of Upland to anchor and unload. Upland was small and rough. Only a few houses clung to the hilly streets. But Upland had been home to a Friends Meeting since 1675. Members had no meetinghouse. They gathered for worship in their homes. These Friends greeted Penn and made him feel comfortable, giving him a place to stay in a town too new to have an inn.

As governor, Penn had the power to name cities and counties, so he renamed Upland after the English city of Chester. He had the power to call a meeting of the new legislature, and he set the date for the first session on December 4. He could make treaties with the

Lenni-Lenape, and legend has it that he first met them that very fall under an elm tree at a place called Shackamaxon.

Penn hoped to learn the Lenni-Lenape language soon, so that the next time they met he "might not want an interpreter." He eagerly studied the way they governed themselves and how the leaders listened to their people. "[N]othing of moment is undertaken, be it war, peace, selling of land or traffic, without advising with them . . . " Penn noted. "It is admirable to consider, how powerful the kings are, and yet how they move by the breath of their people."

During that busy first fall, Penn also traveled to a great new city. At first, it existed mainly in Penn's mind and on paper. He called the city Philadelphia, from the Greek words *philos* (love) and *adelphos* (brother). This city of brotherly love would be located just up the Delaware River. Unlike crowded English cities, Philadelphia would have wide streets with many parks scattered about. Such a plan, Penn hoped, might make it more difficult for diseases, such as smallpox and plague, to spread and ravage the citizens.

When Penn finally arrived by canoe in Philadelphia, ten little houses had sprouted. Streets were being laid out. Penn's vision for a new city was taking shape.

His vision for a fair and just government was slower to develop.

The group of men that met in Chester on December 4, 1682, was disappointingly small. Only half of those invited had shown up. Most who came had no experience running a government. They had run nothing bigger than shops or farms in England. Would they know what to do? William Penn prayed that they would. The men worked together over four days to approve the frame of government Penn had drafted, even daring to suggest a few small changes.

So far Pennsylvania's citizens had done little more than sign off on things presented to them. Could they create their own laws, appoint good judges, and take care of day-to-day government? Penn got part of an answer in the spring. On March 10, 1683, the Assembly and Council met again, this time in Philadelphia. Voices rang out. Fists slammed down on tabletops. The citizens of Pennsylvania lost their tempers as they argued among themselves—and with their governor—over bigger and bolder changes to the frame of government and over new laws. They kept shouting until they'd hammered out a new constitution. It passed on April 2.

In a letter that spring, Penn wrote, "I am mightily taken with this part of the world. . . . I like it so well that . . . I am like to be an adopted American."

But not all of William Penn's dreams came true. Forced to go back to England because of urgent business in 1684, Penn did not return to his adopted home until 1699. That visit was just as short as his first one. Penn was back in England in 1701. By then he was an old man with a gouty leg that pained him and with more troubles and illnesses besides. He lingered on for several years after suffering a stroke in 1712. Early on the morning of July 30, 1718, William Penn died.

Friends remembered him as "a man, a scholar, a Friend." Americans know him as the founder of Pennsylvania. Before all that, however, he was a captain's and an admiral's son. Although he disappointed his father by becoming a Quaker, he didn't let the old admiral down in the end. For those who valued liberty, William Penn was an unofficial ambassador for justice and free and fair trials. For those who suffered for religious freedom, Penn was a minister for openness and tolerance. And for those who, just a few decades after Penn died, would struggle to create a new government for thirteen colonies, much of his blueprint for Pennsylvania became a model to follow.

Selected Bibliography

Dunn, Richard S. and Mary Maples Dunn, eds. *The World of William Penn.* Philadelphia: University of Pennsylvania Press, 1986.

Peare, Catherine Owens. *William Penn: A Biography.* Ann Arbor, MI: The University of Michigan Press, 1956.

Penn, William. *The Papers of William Penn.* Edited by Mary Maples Dunn and Richard S. Dunn, et. al. Philadelphia: University of Pennsylvania Press, 1981.

————. *The Select Works of William Penn.* London: William Phillips, George Yard, Lombard Street, 1825.

Pepys, Samuel. *The Illustrated Pepys: Extracts from the Diary.* Selected & edited by Robert Latham. Berkeley, CA: University of California Press, 1978.

Picard, Liza. *Restoration London: From Poverty to Pets, from Medicine to Magic, from Slang to Sex, from Wallpaper to Women's Rights.* New York: St. Martin's Press, 1997.

Porter, Stephen. *The Great Plague.* Stroud, England: Sutton Publishing, 1999

Street, Lucie. *Uncommon Sailor: A Portrait of Admiral Sir William Penn.* New York: St. Martin's Press, 1988.

Trussell, John B. B. Jr. *William Penn: Architect of a Nation.* Harrisburg, PA: Pennsylvania Historical and Museum Commission, 1998.

Index

Amyraut, Moses, 24

Charles I, King, 8, 11
Chigwell School, 10, 12
Christ Church College, Oxford,
    18, 19, 20, 22, 26
Church of England, 8, 15, 16,
    19, 20, 22, 30
Cromwell, Oliver, 8, 11, 12, 13,
    14, 17

English Civil War, 8–9, 10

Fairfax, 11–12
Fellowship, 7
Fox, George, 47
Frame of Government, The, 52
Friends. *See* Quakerism.

*Great Case of Liberty of
    Conscience, The,* 46

Happy Entrance, 8

Lenni-Lenape Indians, 51, 53,
    57–58
Lincoln's Inn, 26, 27
Loe, Thomas, 15, 16, 29

Macroom Castle, 14, 16
Mead, William, 39–40, 42–43

Naseby, 17–18
New World, 47, 48, 49, 50

Newgate, 44, 45, 47
No Cross, No Crown, 37, 39

Parliament (England), 8–9, 11,
    12, 17, 22, 29, 48
Penn, Bille (William's son), 53
Penn, Letitia (William's
    daughter), 49, 53
Penn, Margaret (William's
    mother), 7, 13, 14, 16, 22
Penn, Peg (William's sister), 11,
    13, 22
Penn, Richard (William's
    brother), 14, 22
Penn, Springett (William's son),
    48, 53, 55
Penn, William: baptism of, 8;
    birth of, 7; death of, 61; and
    disease, 9–10, 28, 45–46, 55,
    58; education of, 10–11, 12,
    13, 14, 18, 19, 22, 24, 26;
    and governance of
    Pennsylvania, 50–52, 53,
    57–59; marriage of, 47, 48,
    49; and Quakerism, 15–16,
    22, 29, 30, 32, 35, 36–37, 39,
    49, 50, 57, 61; relationship
    with father, 12, 13, 14, 15,
    19–20, 22, 25, 26–27, 32–33,
    35, 43, 44, 45, 61; and
    religious freedom, 24, 46, 48,
    52, 61; religious persecution
    of, 36–37, 39–40, 42–43, 44,
    45–46, 47.

CANCELED